Peterson Space Force Base

Through Time

Joseph T. Page II

FONTHILL

This book is dedicated to the men and women of Peterson SFB, securing the High Frontier.

Fonthill Media Inc.
www.fonthill.media
office@fonthillmedia.com

First published 2024

ISBN 978-1-62545-151-4

Typeset in Mrs Eaves XL Serif Narrow
Printed and bound in England

Contents

Acknowledgments

Foremost, I would like to thank my wife and children for their patience through these writing projects, and my "keyboard cats," for typing random characters while walking on the computer keyboard.

A special callout for the enlisted members of the 4th Space Control Squadron (4SPCS) "Space Pirates" (2010–2013) for a raucous time in New Mexico, Las Vegas(!), and Afghanistan. "My" CCS crew did not really require a commissioned officer to run the equipment, but I thank the enlisted cadre (especially the crew chiefs) for letting us think we ran our space control crews. Special thanks to Shadow, Ms. Darlene, and Valkyrie.

I would also like to acknowledge many unnamed Peterson space operators for sharing stories of their time in Colorado Springs. While many of the stories revolved around bureaucratic battles within the hallways of AFSPC Building 1, some of the best "there I was…" tales of uncompromising derring-do took place at various locations around the globe.

Thank you to the Peterson Air and Space Museum cadre and the 21st Space Wing historians for their steadfast determination in preserving the base's history and contributions to national defense.

Eternal gratitude for Alan Sutton, president of Fonthill Media, for allowing another project to highlight United States Air and Space Force history.

Photos are courtesy of the United States Air Force unless otherwise specified.

Introduction

Peterson Space Force Base (SFB) is a United States Space Force (USSF) installation located within the city limits of Colorado Springs, Colorado. The base employs over 7,000 people and occupies approximately 1,300 acres, of which 184 acres are owned by the air force and the remaining are leased from the City of Colorado Springs. Split between the domains of air and space, Peterson SFB contains units from all U.S. military services along with a joint-use airfield shared by the air force and the City of Colorado Springs Municipal Airport as a point of arrival and departure for numerous dignitaries visiting Fort Carson, the Air Force Academy, and NORAD.

World War II and Colorado Springs Army Air Base

The land currently occupied by the base was formerly the site of the Colorado Springs Municipal Airport, beginning aerial operations in 1927. During 1941, the U.S. Army set up a nearby installation at then-Camp Carson and leased the airport for training activities, starting the prolonged relationship between the city and the U.S. military. The army leased the airport runways and buildings before establishing Colorado Springs Army Air Base on April 28, 1942. The base's primary purpose was training crews for photographic reconnaissance under the auspices of the U.S. Army Air Forces (USAAF) Photo Reconnaissance Operational Training Unit, or PROTU. From May 1942 to October 1943, the PROTU trained over twenty combat-ready reconnaissance squadrons for overseas combat operations. One member of the PROTU, 1Lt. Edward J. Peterson, Jr., was killed on August 8, 1942, during take-off prior to a training mission, becoming the second pilot killed in the line of duty at the airfield. The first fatality at the base—2Lt. William H. Borgerding—died one day earlier on August 7 during a plane crash at the airfield. On December 13, 1942, Colorado Springs Army Air Base was renamed Peterson Field after Colorado native son Lt. Peterson. The base was later officially designated Peterson Army Air Field on March 15, 1943.

Construction expanded the base's facilities during 1943 as the U.S. mobilized its wartime efforts, adding training of heavy bomber combat crews to the airfield in October 1943. The 383rd Bombardment Group, relocated from Geiger Field, Washington, became the core of the combat crew training school and its fleet of Consolidated B-24 Liberator heavy bombers. The ten-man Liberator crews trained for three months prior to overseas assignments as replacement crews for war-weary B-24 squadrons. By April 1944, the 383rd Bomb Group was inactivated and replaced by the 214th Army Air Forces Base Unit (Combat Crew Training). Three months later, the base's mission switched to training fighter pilots, with the 268th Army Air Forces Base Unit (Fighter Training Station) training Curtiss P-40 Warhawks aircrews. By April 1945, the establishment of an Army Air Forces Instructor School signaled another shift regarding the changing wartime needs of the USAAF. This mission did not last long, with the War Department closing the base on December 31, 1945, and returning the base property to the City of Colorado Springs.

During the immediate postwar years, Peterson Field was reactivated and inactivated twice: September 29, 1947 to January 15, 1948 and September 22, 1948 to November 7, 1949.

Immediately after birth of the United States Air Force (USAF) on September 18, 1947, the base served as an airfield under Strategic Air Command (SAC), housing the Fifteenth Air Force, which relocated to Colorado Springs in 1946, until the organization's departure to March AFB, California, in 1949. Changes in the global political situation throughout the early Cold War era saw the installation reactivate in early 1951, coincident with the opening of Ent AFB and re-establishment of Air Defense Command, with the base remaining open in the decades since.

Post-World War II Global Threats

The pinnacle of American technological air superiority—the B-29 Superfortress—was touted as a superweapon against the Japanese Empire during World War II, with an extreme range and large payload capabilities. The final days of the war saw specially modified B-29s (code name "Silverplate") drop two atomic weapons on the Japanese cities of Hiroshima and Nagasaki. One country that took notice of the marriage of the B-29 heavy bomber and its atomic payload was the Soviet Union, then allied with the U.S. during the war but not declaring war on Japan until late 1945. During the war, four B-29s made emergency landings in Soviet territory during the Pacific Campaign, with the crews interned, but later being allowed to escape to friendly territory.

These aircraft were dismantled and reverse-engineered into the Tupolev Tu-4 bomber (code name "Bull"), first taking flight on May 19, 1947. By January 1949, it was estimated Long-Range Aviation units (the Soviet version of the U.S. Strategic Air Command) had 250 Tu-4s. On October 18, 1951, mirroring the American B-29s' mission of atomic weapon delivery, a Tu-4 performed the first airdrop test of a Soviet atomic bomb. A macabre joke between American air defense pilots—worried that Soviet Tu-4s would have American markings to confuse U.S. defensive forces—was to look in the window: "If the crew member was pouring coffee out of a Thermos, the bomber was American; but if they were pouring tea out of a samovar [a metal urn], it was Russian."

Cold War Air Defense

On January 1, 1951, the USAF re-established Air Defense Command (ADC), a major command tasked with the air defense of the continental United States (CONUS), Alaska, and Hawaii. The air defense mission had been previously performed by the Continental Air Forces (1944–1946), Air Defense Command (1946–1948), and Continental Air Command (1948–1950). The new command moved to Ent AFB (near downtown Colorado Springs) on January 8, 1951. The establishment of the North American Air Defense Command (NORAD), a bi-national U.S. and Canadian command, saw Peterson Field's importance grow, namely due to lack of flying facilities at Ent AFB. The 4600th Air Base Group was activated at Ent and tasked with administrative, logistical, and facility support for several military commands located in the Colorado Springs area, including Peterson Field. Increase in the group's support mission prompted a redesignation to the 4600th Air Base Wing (4600 ABW) in April 1958.

In April 1975, Ent AFB was shuttered due to urban encroachment and movement of many air defense functions to NORAD's Combat Operations Center inside Cheyenne Mountain. Ent's inactivation saw the 4600 ABW relocate to Peterson Field, redesignated as the 46th Aerospace Defense Wing (46 ADW). On March 1, 1976, Peterson Field's increasing importance was recognized, and the base was renamed Peterson Air Force Base (AFB), with the 46 ADW running the base support mission under the Aerospace Defense Command (ADCOM).

Into the Final Frontier

Changes in the adversary threat—and the advent of thermonuclear-tipped ballistic missiles—saw the importance of air defense merge to become defense in both air and space. Aerospace Defense Command split its forces between Tactical Air Command (manned fighters/interceptor aircraft) and SAC (missile warning and space surveillance) and inactivated in 1979, with Peterson AFB falling under SAC on October 1, 1979.

The growing importance of the space mission area saw the USAF create a new military organization—Space Command—on September 1, 1982, with headquarters at Peterson AFB. The 1st Space Wing was activated on January 1, 1983, and assumed host unit responsibilities from the recently inactivated 46 ADW on April 1, 1983. The 1st Space Wing transferred base operating support responsibilities to a new unit, the 3rd Space Support Wing, in October 1986, but retained the aerospace warning and space surveillance missions. Missile warning radars located around the world fell under the aegis of the wing, as well as space surveillance sites and missile warning satellites.

Post-Cold War Changes at Peterson

In the dramatic post-Cold War drawdown, the USAF attempted to retain units with significant heritage within the service's history. The lineage of the 1st and 3rd Space Wings were not deemed historically significant, and both were inactivated on May 15, 1992, and replaced with the 21st Space Wing (21 SW), a rebranding of a Cold War-era air defense fighter wing relocated from Elmendorf AFB, Alaska. The space warriors of the 21 SW provided missile warning and space control operations to combatant commanders and forces through a worldwide network of ground-based sensors at exotic locations such as:

- Cheyenne Mountain AFS, Colorado
- RAF Fylingdales, United Kingdom
- RAF Feltwell, United Kingdom
- Woomera Air Station, Australia
- Edwards AFB, California
- Moron Air Base, Spain
- Diego Garcia, British Indian Ocean Territory
- Maui, Hawaii
- Choe Jong San, South Korea
- Holloman AFB and White Sands Missile Range, New Mexico
- Sondrestrom Air Base and Thule Air Base, Greenland
- Clear AFS, Alaska
- Cape Cod AFS, Massachusetts
- Robins AFB, Georgia
- Eldorado AFS, Texas
- Cavalier AFS, North Dakota

Peterson's central mission regarding the defense of the United States and North America also involved cooperation between numerous partners, including NORAD, Air Force Reserve Command, and the US Army Space and Missile Defense Command. After the September 11, 2001 attacks on the United States, the newly established U.S. Northern Command (USNORTHCOM) was established on Peterson AFB, relying on the base's expertise with the air and space defense mission.

The establishment of the United States Space Force (USSF) on December 20, 2019 saw the creation of the U.S.'s sixth military service and the inactivation of Air Force Space Command (AFSPC). With the birth of the new military service, Peterson AFB was renamed to Peterson Space Force Base on July 26, 2021.

DEFENSE OF THE NATION THROUGH AIR AND SPACE DOMAINS: The emblem of the 46th Aerospace Defense Wing displays the elements of a castle battlements (parapets) at the base, with stylized arched contrails of three rockets and two aircraft in flight, representing the unit's mission of stalwart support for the aerospace defense mission.

1

Lieutenant Edward J. Peterson, Jr.

Edward Joseph Peterson, Jr. was born in Harlan County, Nebraska, on November 16, 1917 into a family of farmers. After his family settled in Colorado, he spent his formative years in Loveland and Berthoud, until his family moved to Denver in 1931. Graduating fifth in his class from Englewood High School in 1935, Peterson attended Denver University, graduating in 1939 with a Bachelor of Arts degree in education and a Master of Arts degree in 1940. While at university, Peterson became interested in aviation and enrolled in the Civilian Pilot Training Program (CPTP) at the Walt Higley Flying School. From 1938 until 1944, the CPTP (renamed War Training Service in 1942) signed up civilians into the Army Air Forces Enlisted Reserve which allowed trainees to attend college and take private flying lessons with an agreement to enter military service after graduation. In March 1941, Peterson enlisted in the U.S. Army's Aviation Cadet Program and entered pilot training. He earned his wings and a commission in the USAAF in October 1941—just two months shy of the December 7, 1941 and the Japanese sneak attack on Pearl Harbor (HI). (*Peterson Air and Space Museum*)

EDWARD AND RUTH, LOVERS IN FLIGHT: Peterson met his future wife Ruth (1920–1995) while in the Civilian Pilot Training Program. Ruth Peterson (*née* Wallrich), a native of Alamosa, Colorado, was the first licensed woman pilot at Adams State College and completed training with fourteen male students. Ruth—as described in a 1940 news clipping—was "a typical and modern American co-ed," as well as being an expert swimmer, tennis player, and skier as well as editor of her college newspaper and member of a dramatic club. Edward and Ruth were married on March 17, 1941—only two days before he was ordered to report for basic flight training at Stockton Field, California. (*Peterson Air and Space Museum*)

PETERSON'S RISE THROUGH THE RANKS: After graduating from flight training on October 31, 1941, Cadet Peterson was commissioned as a second lieutenant in the USAAF and immediately assigned to fly P-38 Lightning fighter aircraft. Considered an outstanding pilot, Peterson was promoted to first lieutenant on February 1, 1942 and reassigned to the 14th Photographic Reconnaissance Squadron (14 PRS) at Colorado Springs Army Air Base. Here Lt. Peterson holds his cocker spaniel, Honey, who often accompanied him on his flights. As an expert pilot, Peterson was often the squadron's *de facto* test pilot after aircraft maintenance work. He was placed as the 14 PRS' operations officer on July 26, 1942. (*Peterson Air and Space Museum*)

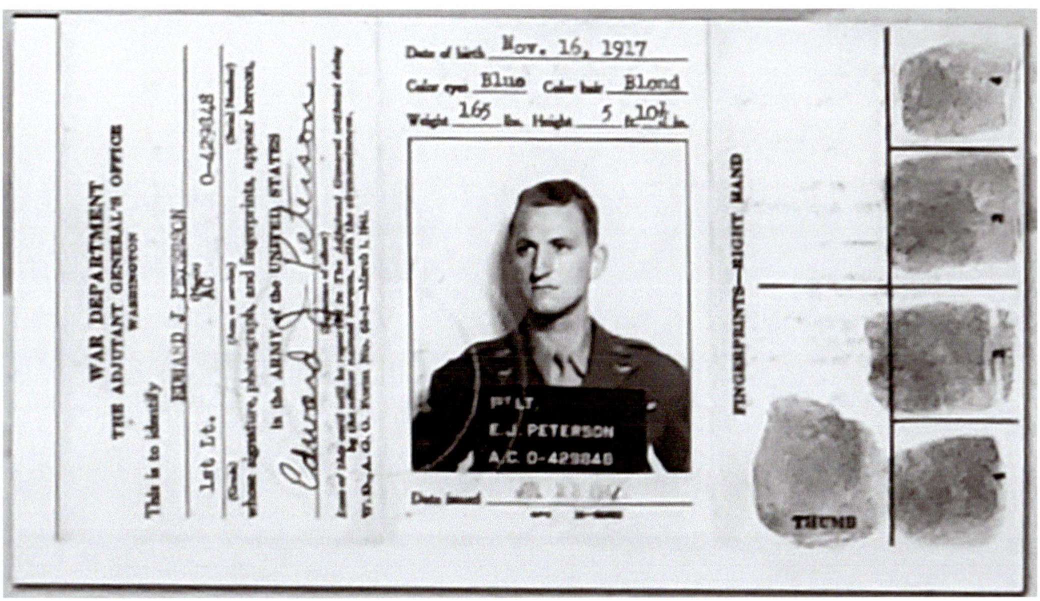

WAR DEPARTMENT
THE ADJUTANT GENERAL'S OFFICE
WASHINGTON

This is to identify EDWARD J. PETERSON
1st Lt. (Grade) AC (Arm or service) 0-429848 (Serial Number)
whose signature, photograph, and fingerprints, appear hereon,
in the ARMY of the UNITED STATES
Edward J. Peterson (Signature of officer)

Date of birth Nov. 16, 1917
Color eyes Blue Color hair Blond
Weight 165 lbs. Height 5 ft. 10½ in.

Date issued

FINGERPRINTS—RIGHT HAND

THUMB

PLANE VICTIM

FIRST LT. ED PETERSON

Well known Englewood boy who was recently fatally injured in an army airplane crash at Colorado Springs.

FAREWELL TO AN AERIAL WARRIOR: On Saturday, August 8, 1942, Lt. Peterson took off on a routine aircraft flight following an engine replacement. Immediately after lifting off the runway, the left engine of his Lockheed P-38 Lightning failed and Peterson crashed with the aircraft bursting into flames upon impact. A three-man crash rescue crew pulled Peterson out of the burning aircraft, and he was taken to Glockner (now Penrose) Hospital. Suffering extensive burns on his head, chest, and lower body, Peterson faded in and out of consciousness while asking how this would affect his future flying ability. Around 3 p.m., Peterson succumbed to his injuries. While his wife Ruth was notified about the crash, she was unable to reach him before he died. At his widow's request, Peterson's remains were cremated and scattered over Pike's Peak, Denver, and Alamosa from an F-4 aircraft. On December 13, 1942, Colorado Springs Army Air Base was renamed Peterson Field. Artifacts, such as this memorial plaque, and news clippings adorn the entryway to the Peterson Air and Space Museum. (*Peterson Air and Space Museum*)

2

Colorado Springs Army Air Base and Peterson Field

Prior to World War II, the tourist draw to Colorado Springs was the high altitude, dry atmosphere, and clear, sunny days—all characteristics that make for excellent flying. Here, the "Manassa Mauler," professional boxer William Harrison "Jack" Dempsey (second from right) arrives at the Colorado Springs airport on May 29, 1930. He is joined by (left to right) his manager Mr. Leonard Sacks, and philanthropists Mr. Spencer and Mrs. Julie Penrose. Born in Manassa (CO), Dempsey found great success as a boxer, with his popularity leading to the sport's first million dollar "gate"—the sum of money taken during a sporting venue's sale of tickets—during a bout on July 2, 1921 in Jersey City (NJ). In the early 1940s, as the winds of war were approaching, Colorado Springs transportation hubs were crowded with both visiting tourists and military troops moving toward training bases outside the state. Local officials took notice and brought the area's positive environmental factors to the Army Air Corps' attention. (*Peterson Air and Space Museum*)

LEAST BOMB-ABLE CITY IN THE UNITED STATES: The January 16, 1942 issue of *TIME* magazine declared that Colorado Springs was the "... least bombable city in the United States," equating the near impossibility of an enemy attacking by air. Nearly six months earlier, the city received an announcement that Colorado Springs was chosen as a site for a "large Army cantonment," which became Camp (later Fort) Carson. The top image shows the beautiful clear skies in September 1940 that drew the (then) Army Air Corps to investigate the area between the Southern Rocky Mountains and the Great Plains physiographic provinces.

ART DECO FOR THE AERODROME: Built between 1940 and 1941, the Colorado Springs Municipal Airport passenger terminal (present day building 981) was built in the Art Deco architectural style, showcasing simple, streamlined look with its stucco-covered brick. Ceramic tiles, decorated in an Egyptian bird motif, adorn the building with fluted columns and stepped facades. Built by W. T. Mitchell and Son for $19,875 (1940 dollars), the building only served its civilian masters for a brief time before the grounds became subsumed by the arriving military operations. When the military took over in 1941, the airport's runways and taxiways were demolished, *in lieu* of newer runways built by military engineers and the Works Progress Administration (WPA).

BASE CONSTRUCTION BEGINS: This early view shows the area engineer's office (stone building to right) located near the contractor facilities (black tarpaper buildings with multiple windows), with a Piper L-4A Grasshopper sitting in a parking area. The Orman Construction Company offices (far left) sit near the infirmary (far center) and the base gymnasium (right). Both facilities—gym and infirmary—are part of the initial phases of construction at most military installations, as they are key to any military training environment to care for fitness and injured soldiers.

THE EVER-CHANGING AIRFIELD: Construction cruised along as military training continued. To care for the spiritual welfare of the soldiers, military installations established houses of worship. The Colorado Springs Army Air Base Chapel completed construction during the first week in September 1942, holding its first services only mere days later. The main entrance to the airfield shows a sign proudly proclaiming its new name, memorializing Lt. Peterson after his sudden accidental death on August 8, 1942.

AND THE ARMY (CONSTRUCTION) GOES ROLLING ALONG: Since the early days of the war, the installation was constantly being revised and supplemented with the expansion of the garrison's mission and additional commitments brought to the field. In this 1943 photo, construction continues at Peterson Field as Pikes Peak looms in the background. Building 365 undergoes construction as well as the hangers in the rear of the photograph. With PROTU's photographic training mission increasing, Army Corps of Engineers directed contractors (pausing for the photographer) to add a new wing to the base photograph laboratory (adjacent to building T-345) in the middle of 1943.

TWO SIDES OF THE AERIAL "COIN": Soldiers operate a crew-served 0.50-caliber M2 Browning water-cooled machine gun during anti-aircraft training at Peterson Field in 1943. John Browning's gun designs were adapted by the U.S. military to perform a variety of roles upon a cornucopia of weapons platforms during World War II. Anti-aircraft defense made the difference between life and death for soldiers during most combat operations, as the Allies did not gain air superiority until late in the war. A snow-covered ramp displays the nose of a parked B-17 Flying Fortress during a typical Colorado winter day. Early PROTU operations saw aging B-25 Mitchell bombers fly out of the airfield along with F-4 (photographic P-38s), and B-17 Flying Fortresses.

B-24 LIBERATORS AT PETERSON FIELD: Both images show B-24 Liberators at Peterson Field, after the changeover from PROTU to the 383rd Bomb Group in October 1943, as a Replacement Training Unit (RTU) for individual aircrews heading to combat. Going into production in 1941 and learning from other heavy bomber projects, the B-24 carried a larger bomb load coupled with a larger combat radius than the B-17 Flying Fortress. This made the aircraft desirable for long-range bombardment, but its lack of armament and armor made it a poor substitute for the B-17 in aerial combat against the blood-thirsty Luftwaffe (German Air Force). The ten-man crew stands in front of their likely B-24J variant, identified by the up-angled pitot tubes (above standing crewman on far right) and Consolidated A-6 nose gun turret. The ramp image shows a B-24D parked in front of a taxiing P-47D Thunderbolt with a "razorback" canopy. Women Airforce Service Pilots (WASPs) were the first to bring the P-47 to Peterson Field, delivering six aircraft in 1943.

FIGHTERS AND "FOTO" BIRDS AT PETERSON FIELD: Maintainers inspect a F-4 (P-38 Lightning) while a refueling truck sits in front of the aircraft. On April 28, 1942, the Photographic Reconnaissance Operational Training Unit (PROTU) was activated at the Colorado Springs Municipal Airport prior to the opening (and renaming) of Colorado Springs Army Air Base. Before PROTU's consolidated training, photo-reconnaissance pilot trainees received piecemeal training on their modified P-38 Lightning aircraft—designated F-4s, with "F" phonetically representing "Foto"—before shipping out to the European Theater of Operations. Rows of B-24 Liberator bombers sit parked in the background. The air base transitioned to P-40 flying instruction under the 72nd Fighter Wing around July 1944, with this Warhawk pilot looking out of their open canopy prior to take-off. The P-40 was the third-most produced American fighter during World War II—after the P-51 and P-47—and was provided to the British and Soviets under the names "Tomahawk" (original P-40 and the B and C variants) and "Kittyhawk" (P-40D and later variants).

OTHER MISSIONS ON THE AIR BASE: Maintenance trainees inspect the engine of a P-40 Warhawk inside a Peterson Field hangar. Six of the twelve cylinders inside the Allison V-1710 engine are seen above the number "35." Potential fighter/pursuit aircraft mechanics were identified after taking the Army General Classification Test (AGCT) and sent to a basic aircraft maintenance course at Chanute Field (IL) or Sheppard Field (TX) with follow-on training at factory schools at the aircraft manufacturing plants. The former passenger terminal was first used as an Army/Red Cross Emergency Relief Center in June 1943. Here, the terminal fills the role as "Station Headquarters," with three olive-drab staff vehicles out front.

FILM DEVELOPMENT FOR THE ARMY AIR FORCES: During an address presenting a photogrammetric award in 1944, General Henry "Hap" Arnold stated, "Often a camera mounted in a P-38 has proved of greater importance than a P-38 with its normal complement of guns," underscoring the importance of aerial reconnaissance. The F-4 aircraft—P38s modified for photo-reconnaissance—had twin 24-inch cameras and a 6-inch trimetrogon camera (aerial photographic survey method with one camera is pointed directly downwards, and two angled 30 degrees off the flight path) installed in the nose. An instructor teaches students on the parts and pieces of a K-17 camera assembly. Until October 1, 1943, every photo-reconnaissance unit member in the USAAF received training at Peterson Field. Here soldiers pose in front of the base photographic laboratory (building T-320) on June 12, 1944.

THE LOCAL "WATERING HOLE" FOR MILITARY MEMBERS: Enlisted members enjoy a frosty beverage at the newly opened sergeants' club. The need for a location for enlisted military members to relax and unwind came up early in the base's history around August 1942. The sergeants' club allowed membership from the "first four grades": master sergeant (grade 1), technical sergeant (grade 2), staff sergeant (grade 3), and sergeant (grade 4). The outside of the officers' club (building T-1457), seen here in June 1943, offers a bit of refinement with the multiple outward opening doors lined with curtains. Membership in the club is an oft-expectation of the officer corps, as reported in the 1942 record all officers were members of the club, with monthly dues of $3 (equivalent to $58.61 USD in 2023).

THE PETERSON OFFICER'S CLUB: The officers' club had spacious seating, a snack bar ($0.25 malts, $0.20 sandwiches, with Coke and parfaits) and a bar decorated with exotic (false) palm trees, forecasting locations the officers were likely to ship out to in the Pacific theater. The basement of the officers' club held the cashier's booth. The cage's metal bars, seen here in April 1943, had a historical connection to the region, originally belonging to the Colorado Springs Mining Exchange before its dissolution in the early 1920s.

FEEDING THE FORCE, PART 1: Food preparation specialists, also known as "cooks," learn their craft inside a large classroom. Meat preparation, with all the hazards of contamination and spoilage, took center stage on this particular instruction day. Students learned "The Functions of Food in Nutrition," as well how to roast meat, and then carve it after cooking. With over 5,000 troops on base at the end of 1943, keeping the force fed was an impressive logistical feat. Sides of beef sit in the freezer facilities at the commissary in February 1943, awaiting the deft touches from the food preparation cadre.

FEEDING THE FORCE, PART 2: Each food preparatory location had unique skills the kitchen staff had to learn. Here, a master sergeant instructs soldiers on the proper usage of metal utensils and food storage containers. Pyramidal tents, such as these, were used by base bakers to make bread for the Peterson Field troops. Occasionally, tents were knocked down during strong gusts as shown here after such windstorm in January 1943.

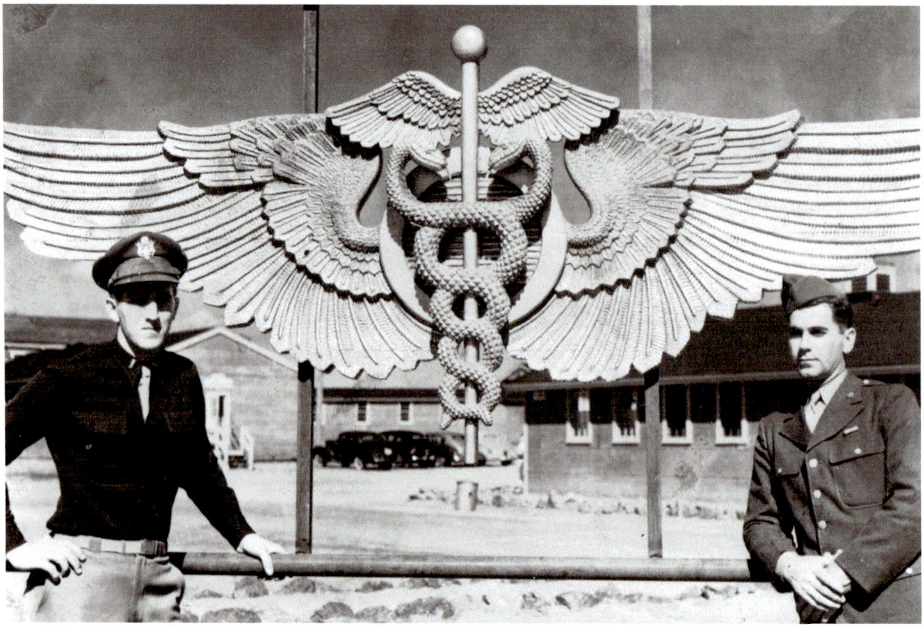

PETERSON'S MEDICAL FORCE: Two unidentified soldiers pose in front of the U.S. Army Medical Corps caduceus insignia outside of the base hospital. In Greek mythology, the caduceus ("herald's staff") was originally associated with commerce and negotiation and was carried by Hermes, and in Roman myths, Mercury. Whether chosen by ignorance or accident, the symbol shown here (two snakes intertwined around a staff) misrepresented medicine when chosen by the U.S. Army medical practitioners in the mid-1800s. The Rod of Asclepius, with one snake coiled around a staff (associated with Hippocrates, the "father of medicine"), is the traditional symbol for medicine. Base surgeons and nurses, seen here during the first operation at Peterson Field hospital, perform a resection of a pilonidal cyst on February 20, 1943. Nearby Camp Carson allotted ninety-eight beds to Peterson soldiers up to 1943, however, the army surgeon general requested construction of a 180-bed ward for the air base's hospital.

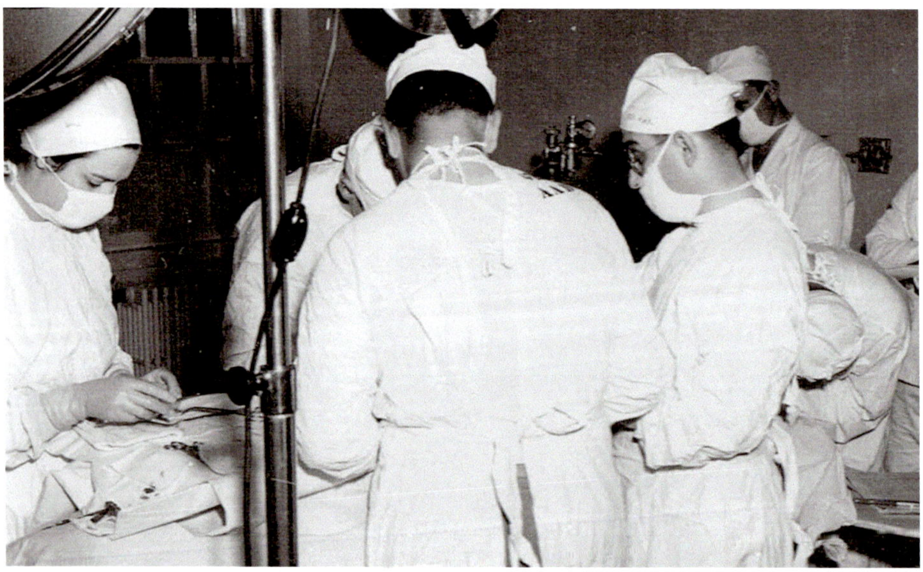

THE FEMININE INFLUX OF PETERSON WOMEN'S ARMY CORPS: The Peterson history for this timeframe states "...Peterson Field on June 7, 1943, showed the beginning of a feminine influx," with the activation of the 795th WAC Post Headquarters Company. Here, the 1945 post-war WAC cadre from the 268th Base Unit's Squadron "B" pose for a unit photo on September 5, 1945. The WAC detachment members performed various duties at the base, such as administrative and communications work, and supply and transportation as well as working at Second Air Force headquarters, near downtown Colorado Springs. In 1944, enlisted WAC communications specialists earned their flight qualifications and were assigned as radio operators on cargo aircraft flying missions from Peterson Field. Amid the hustle and bustle of the training base, the dayroom of the Peterson Hospital provides a relaxing space for convalescent patients with comfortable chairs and plenty of reading material.

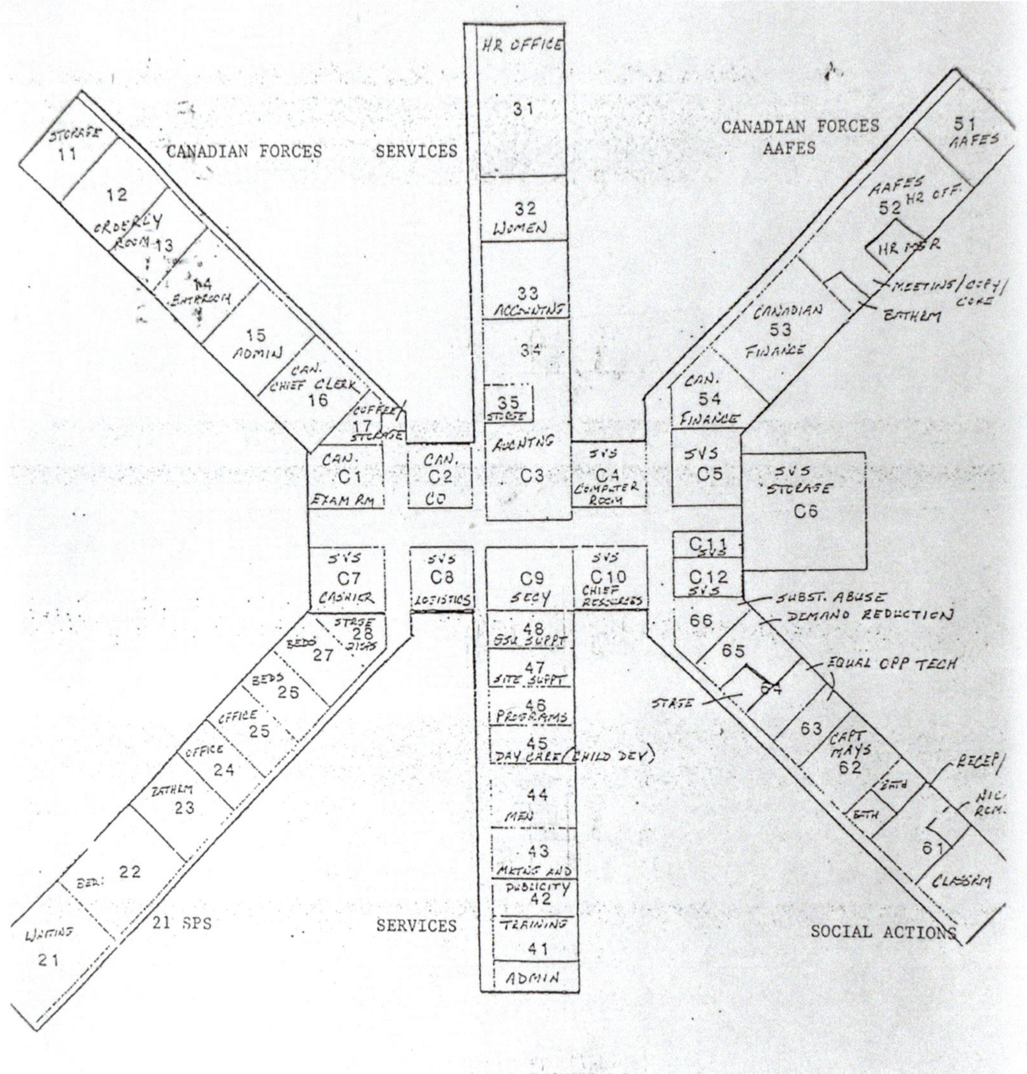

"Spiders" Inhabiting Peterson Army Air Field: Building 880, colloquially known as "The Spider Building," was part of the initial building phase of the base in 1942 and was finished by 1943. The exceptional building held a photographic unit—the 6th Photographic Squadron—with the unique mission of creating accurate flight charts and detailed maps from aerial photography. Some of the prized productions from the photographic squadron (prior to their move to Colorado Springs) include maps for Lt. Col. James "Jimmy" Doolittle's raid on Tokyo in April 1942. During the interwar years, building 880 was leased to a local chicken farmer, with the building obtaining some apocryphal mentions as "the turkey farm." Post poultry producing and processing, the building held a menagerie of functions such as army dormitory; morale, welfare, and recreation; security forces correctional custody facility; Canadian Armed Forces members; Army and Air Force Exchange Service (AAFES); base child development center; and as the base package liquor store.

BUILDING 880 AND MAPPING FOR THE WAR EFFORT: An aerial view of building 880, "the Spider Building," belies the work of photogrammetry specialists inside the structure. Members of the 6th Photographic Squadron work on creation of maps and charts for the armed forces during World War II. This squadron used aerial photography—drawn from "foto-reconnaissance" aircraft such as the F-4, F-5, F-7, and F-10—to produce accurate navigation charts and detailed maps. The Peterson Air and Space Museum contains a thorough display of the squadron, to include the unit emblem and mascot, "Nicky the Owl." Nothing remains of Building 880 today but a vacant field off of Ent Avenue and Suffolk Street, as the building was demolished in 2010.

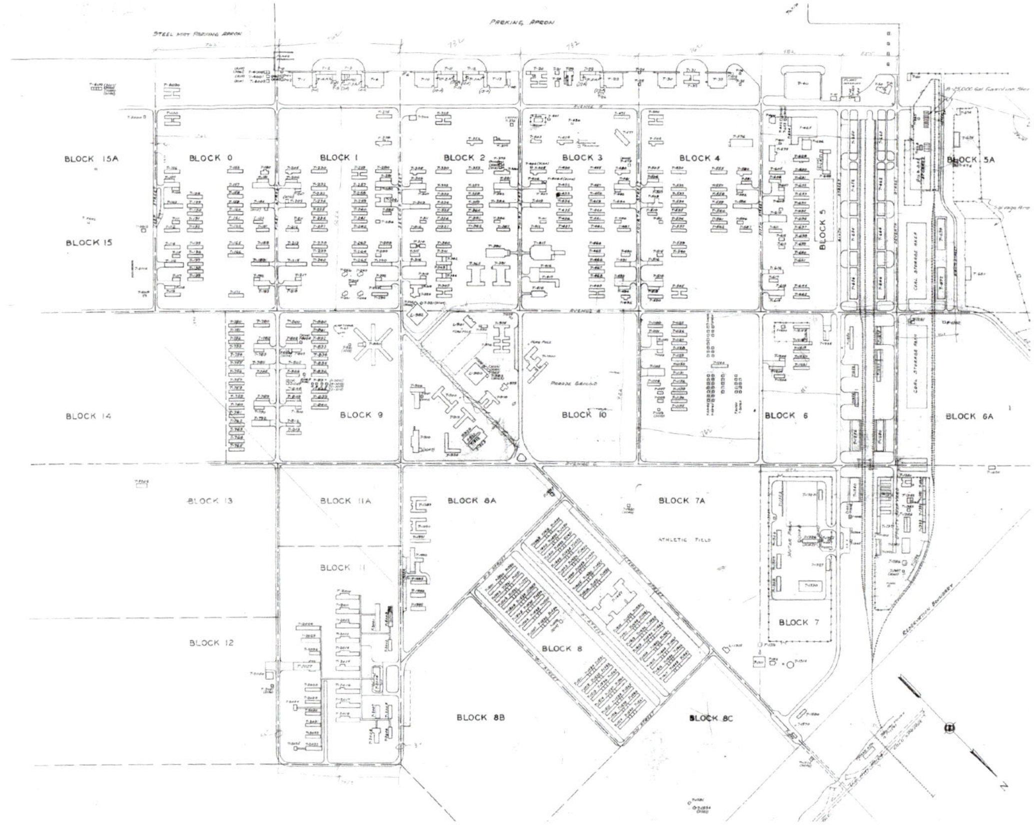

Map of Peterson Army Air Field: On this 1945 map of Peterson Army Air Field, the "Spider Building" (building 880) can be easily spotted (near the center left), as well as the parking ramp for aircraft at the top of the image. The base inactivation in December 1945 and subsequent reactivations throughout the rest of the decade, and final reactivation in 1951 saw many of these buildings remain to support Cold War air defense among other missions. Examples of these buildings survived through the end of the twentieth century, with building 880 being demolished in 2010, sixty-eight years after construction!

3

Cold War Air Defense

After the destruction of the Japanese cities of Hiroshima and Nagasaki from atomic weapons during World War II, many questions remained about how future military forces would operate through an atomic conflict. Conceived days after the end of World War II, Operation Crossroads became the first large-scale nuclear test series against military hardware, such as naval warships, with three explosions ("shots") planned—Able, Baker, and Charlie. Shot Able was air-dropped by a B-29 Superfortress onto a naval fleet of ninety-five target ships on July 1, 1946. Able's full effects were mitigated, however, by the bomb missing its aim point by 2,130 feet. On July 25, 1946, shot Baker, shown here, was detonated 90 feet underwater, carving a 30-foot-deep, 2,000-foot-wide crater within the surface of the sea floor. The blast effects, seen here as a giant geyser, blew nearly 2 million tons of water into the air to a height of approximately one mile and creating a 94-foot-high tidal wave. Between the nine ships sinking due to the shockwave and falling water, the blast spread radioactive water all over the remaining surface ships, causing such an unimaginable disaster that the third test—shot Charlie—was cancelled.

MIRROR IMAGES OF NUCLEAR HORROR: Countering the threat of the Soviet's growing bomber fleet, the USAF re-established Air Defense Command in 1951, moving its headquarters from Mitchel Field (NY) to Ent AFB near downtown Colorado Springs. This Tu-4 Bull Soviet bomber was a bolt-by-bolt duplicate of an American B-29 Superfortress bomber, right down to the rivet patterns in the wings. Appearing in 1947, the Tu-4 bomber was used during a 1951 test of an air-dropped atomic bomb, likely mirroring the Mark III "Fatman" device developed by the Americans to end World War II. This capability alerted U.S. war planners to the Soviet's threatening intent in the postwar era. With the establishment of the North American Air Defense Command (NORAD) on September 12, 1957, Ent AFB became the headquarters location, with Peterson Field providing support. Here, members from the four U.S. military services and one Canadian representative stand in formation. Note the forty-eight-star U.S. flag, dating the photo between 1957 and 1959.

INSIDE THE HEART OF EARLY AMERICAN AIR DEFENSE: Map projections show the world situation inside NORAD's Combat Operations Center within the Chidlaw Building *circa* 1964. The far-right screen places North America as the focal point, while the left-hand screen uses a modified polar projection to show the location of Soviet forces.

On March 7, 1963, the building was dedicated to General Benjamin W. Chidlaw, honoring the former commander of the USAF's Air Defense Command and the Joint Service Continental Air Defense Command. Built as a stopgap until the Cheyenne Mountain Complex was completed, the 300,000-square-foot Childlaw Building contained three floors (one underground), an auditorium seating 174 people, and cooling and heating systems to maintain the workers and computer systems. As the headquarters of NORAD and prime command and control for the Semi-Automatic Ground Environment (SAGE) air defense system, the Childlaw Building was identified as Node Number 1 on NORAD's alert network. On April 20, 1966, the Combat Operations Center responsibilities transferred from Ent AFB/ Childlaw Building to the Cheyenne Mountain Complex. The building remained contracted to the U.S. government until the 1993, when it was sold to a telecommunications company.

STAFF SERGEANT JOSE R. "MARK" ARAGON, HOMETOWN HERO: This hometown hero's story is part of the wonderful tapestry of Peterson's history. S/Sgt. Mark Aragon graduated from Fountain High School (CO) in 1956 and joined the air force soon afterwards. Trained as a jet engine mechanic, Aragon served at assignments in Texas, Nevada, Italy, and Colorado Springs (Ent and Peterson), before taking a ninety-day temporary duty assignment at Bien Hoa Air Base, Vietnam. Aragon lost his life on May 16, 1965, during heroic actions to save lives on the flight line after several 500-pound bombs accidentally exploded while B-57B Canberra bombers were taxiing for take-off. Aragon assisted wounded comrades and helped clear the flight line of equipment that could ignite or explode before one of the secondary blasts caused injuries resulting in his death. Aragon was posthumously awarded the Bronze Star and left behind a wife and two children. Aircraft mechanics at Peterson Field (*circa* 1965) work on the engines of a C-54 Skymaster belonging to Military Air Transportation Command, the forerunner to the Cold War-era Military Airlift Command (MAC) and today's Air Mobility Command (AMC).

FLIGHT OPERATIONS AT PETERSON FIELD: Between January 1, 1951, and February 28, 1975, the base commander of Ent AFB also commanded Peterson Field and the 4600th Air Base Wing. The situation reversed itself in 1975, when Ent became an annex to Peterson AFB. Before Ent AFB closed and became an annex, Peterson Field provided support to the base's various military organizations, including flight operations and distinguished visitor (DV) engagements. The nighttime image shows the air traffic control tower and base operations, with civilian aircraft on the parking apron. This T-33 Shooting Star aircraft (s/n 58-0509) was assigned to Brigadier General Michael J. Ingelido, the Air Defense Command inspector general *circa* 1964/1965 for transport duties to other ADC bases. The airframe now resides at the Jackson County Airport in Jackson (MI) in its ADC livery.

PETERSON'S EXPANDING INFLUENCE: World War II-era hangars designated T-30 (far left), T-33 (left center), and T40 (center right) sit near the flight line in 1970. Existing at the time as a support base to Ent AFB's Air Defense Command, Peterson's air traffic numbers remained high, providing visitors to the U.S. Air Force Academy, Cheyenne Mountain Complex, and Ent AFB with a landing strip. Inside of an Air Transport Clinic, flight surgeon Colonel (Dr.) Edward Crane examines a civilian patient. The Peterson Clinic performed this type of field training once a year to remain current on skills required in deployable situations. Note the shoulder patch of the 46th Aerospace Defense Wing, which replaced the 4600th Air Base Wing for base operations functions, dating this image between 1975 and 1983.

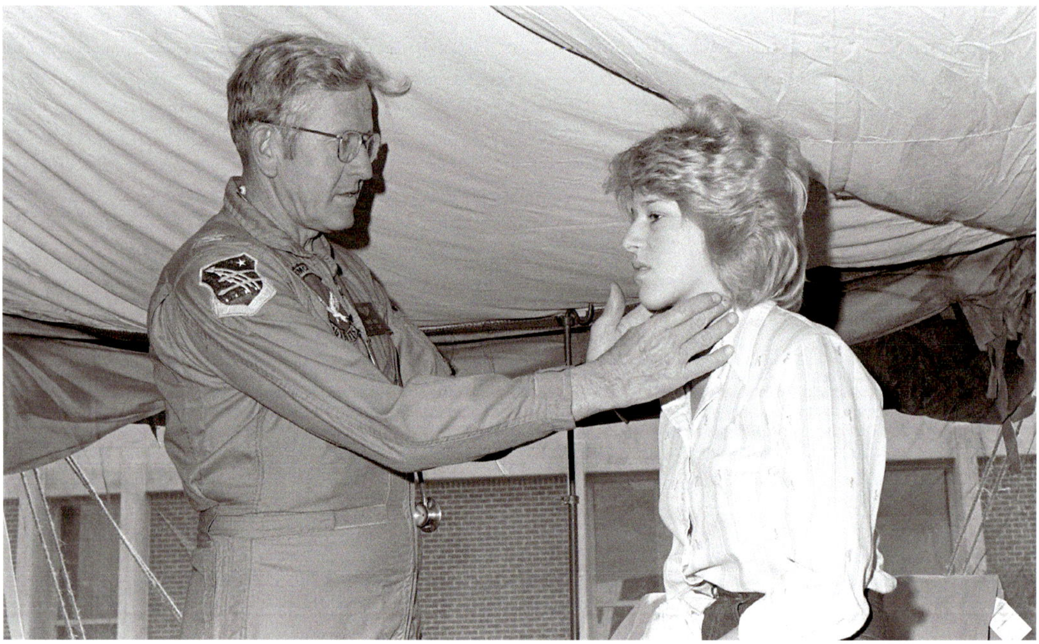

BOB HOPE VISITS, WHILE MARKSMEN FIND THEIR TARGETS: Col. Glenn A. Griffith, vice commander of the 46th Aerospace Defense Wing, welcomes Bob Hope on arrival at Peterson AFB in 1983. Bob Hope's connection with the base stretches back to 1943, when he, Bing Crosby, Ed Dudley, and Lewis B. Maytag played an exhibition round of golf at the Broadmoor Hotel. The event proceeds collected went towards building a driving range at then-Peterson Army Air Field. Base security police practice firing their M-16A1 rifles at targets with an over-the-barricade stance. The 15th Regional Marksmanship competition was held at the base on September 11, 1981.

A Moment in Time Tells the Tale: A security police man takes aim with his M-16A1 rifle from the kneeling position during the 15th Regional Marksmanship matches held at Peterson AFB, September 11, 1981. Two notable features in this photograph are the Strategic Air Command (SAC) crest on his beret, and his three stripes (and visible star) on his subdued shoulder rank. In 1979, the renamed-Aerospace Defense Command (ADCOM) inactivated, and the mission assets were split between Tactical Air Command (TAC), gaining the interceptors and remaining air warning radar stations, and SAC gaining missile warning and space surveillance installations. Peterson's 46th Aerospace Defense Wing realigned under SAC from 1979 until 1983, until the standup of Air Force Space Command (AFSPC). The three chevrons and star on his shoulder insignia denote this man as a sergeant (E-4). From 1976 through 1991, the fourth enlisted grade rank (E-4) was split as a senior airman (SrA), with a nearly invisible star in the center of the chevron, and sergeant (colloquially known as a "Buck Sergeant"), with a visible star. The rank difference did not offer greater pay; however, it provided the sergeant a promotion in responsibility, making them members of the non-commissioned officer (NCO) corps, able to take on supervisory and leadership roles over airmen, their former peers.

4

Into the Final Frontier

Based on fears of losing control of the "High Ground" of space to the Soviets and organizational mismanagement of space-related operations within non-operational air force commands, U.S. Air Force Chief of Staff General Lew Allen, Jr., announced the creation of a space command organization at a Pentagon press conference on June 20, 1982. The new command—initially given the job of coordinating only air force activities in space—was established as Space Command (SPACECOM) on September 1, 1982. Bolstered by the Reagan Administration's Strategic Defense Initiative, the White House supported the creation of unified military space organization coordinating efforts between all services. The 1982-originated organization was renamed Air Force Space Command (AFSPC) on November 15, 1985, while the unified combatant command was activated as United States Space Command (USSPACECOM) on September 23, 1985. This early rendition of the air force's "Space Command" (1982–1985) logo displays the words in yellow. The subsequent renaming to AFSPC saw the logo change with extra words and a blue font color. The delta emblem in the middle would become a frequent characteristic of later space-related organizational emblems.

ESTABLISHMENT OF UNITED STATES SPACE COMMAND, PART 1: On September 1, 1982, the USAF established Space Command at Peterson AFB (CO). An unidentified senior airman and staff sergeant from the USAF Academy Color Guard unfurl the new Space Command flag as Under Secretary of the Air Force Edward C. Aldridge, Jr., (left center), Air Force Vice Chief of Staff General Jerome E. O'Malley (center), and General James V. Hartinger, the first commander of the newly formed Space Command, look on while standing at attention on stage. Under Secretary of the Air Force Edward "Pete" Aldridge, Jr., gives the opening address at the ceremony. Aldridge's selection to speak at the event is notable, not due to his public job title, but another classified title he held at the time: director of the National Reconnaissance Office (NRO). The director of the NRO is responsible to the secretary of defense for all national space and assigned airborne reconnaissance activities. In this capacity, Aldridge was slated to become a payload specialist on STS-62A, the first shuttle mission from Vandenberg AFB (CA), and a likely NRO-dedicated mission. After the Space Shuttle *Challenger* disaster in January 1986, the flight was cancelled and all shuttle-related facilities at Vandenberg were placed in "operational caretaker status." (*National Archives*)

ESTABLISHMENT OF UNITED STATES SPACE COMMAND, PART 2: USAF Gen. James V. Hartinger signs his first special order as commander of the recently formed Space Command (SPACECOM), while Under Secretary of the Air Force Edward C. Aldridge, Jr., (right) and Air Force Vice Chief of Staff General Jerome E. O'Malley (left) look on. The North Gate of Peterson AFB states the base is "Home of The Space Command" on April 1, 1984, with Pikes Peak looming in the background. Pikes Peak's height and proximity to the Great Plains often made it the first sight of westward bound wagon trains. In July 1893, Katharine Lee Bates penned the song "America the Beautiful" after admiring the view from the top of the peak. While the base sign's braggadocio would hold true into 1985, the sign's display would later be altered to make the distinction between the Air Force Space Command and the United States Space Command, after the latter organization's standup. (*National Archives*)

Elements of the Past Guide the Present: Due to Ent AFB's small size, a construction boom on Peterson started in 1967. Building 1470, pictured here, was originally constructed in 1969 to house wing personnel for Air Defense Command inside its 47,000-square-foot structure. When Ent AFB's pending closure was announced in 1974, a 41,000-square-foot mirror-image addition was built onto building 1470 (appropriately designated as building 1471). After Ent AFB closed in 1975, ADC and NORAD were reassigned to Peterson AFB, though the organizations continued to be physically located at an off-site facility leased from the City of Colorado Springs. Here, in the early 1980s, the Ent Building held the personnel of the 1st Space Wing. In 1987–1988, headquarters for the newly created U.S. Space Command and NORAD were moved into the building 1470. HQ NORAD would remain until March 2003, until it moved to building 2. The heraldic emblem of the 1st Space Wing displays two uneven ellipses representing both low and high orbital paths traced by satellites and two yellow rays depicting space surveillance and communications capability from ground base sensors. The 1st Space Wing would administer the core space surveillance and missile warning units from 1983 to 1992, when the unit was inactivated and replaced by the 21st Space Wing.

CONSTRUCTION OF BUILDING 1: In 1985, plans were approved for a new combined headquarters building to be built on Peterson—the first new headquarters building constructed in the USAF in two decades. Building 1 was constructed as a 250,000-square-foot, three-story office building constructed of glass and steel. The appearance of the building was designed to symbolize the high-tech mission of Space Command with a futuristic look.

INSIDE PETERSON'S BUILDING 1: An increasing fad in the 1980s was the pretense of healthy eating with availability of salad bars for restaurant patrons. Air force eating establishments followed these trends, with the food area inside building 1 included one of these salad setups, along with a grilled food area (right). An internal shot of a sitting area inside building 1 shows the intimate setup of chairs and plenty of natural lighting. Air Force Space Command personnel moved into building 1 from the Chidlaw Building around November–December 1987. In 2003, building 1 was dedicated to the memory of Gen. James Hartinger, who was the first commander of Air Force Space Command.

A GLASS AND STEEL FUTURE: An internal shot inside building 1 shows the three-story office building aspect. The increasing use of natural lighting inside coupled with a sleek design of steel and glass gave a futuristic feel to the headquarters of air force space operations. The aerial south-facing view of building 1 shows ample parking spaces for the AFSPC staff members. The eastward parking lots were eliminated in 2002 with the construction of building 2 (Eberhard-Findley Building, home of NORAD and U.S. Northern Command) and building 3 (home of U.S. Army Space and Missile Defense Command). Present-day parking is still a beast, but now there is more office space to work in.

SUPPORT FOR COLORADO SPRINGS SPACE UNITS: The emblem of the 3rd Space Support Wing shows the typical space elements of a globe and orbital paths held up by pillars, exemplifying the mission of the organization. The wing was an active-duty unit of AFSPC from 1986 to 1992, providing administration of space units at nearby Cheyenne Mountain Complex, Onizuka AFB (CA), Thule, and Sondrestrom Air Bases in Greenland. The unit was disestablished in 1992, when the 21st Space Wing assumed host unit duties at Peterson AFB. A photo of the entrance building to the Cheyenne Mountain Complex, located at Cheyenne Mountain AFS (CO), states the two main organizations at the site, NORAD and "the" (AF) Space Command on April 1, 1984. Many support functions within Cheyenne Mountain rely on personnel and equipment from Peterson AFB.

THE UNITED STATES' NORTHERNMOST MILITARY BASE: The nearly 10,000-foot runway at Thule Air Base, Greenland (08T/26T) runs in a northeast–southwest orientation toward North Star Bay. Since 1961, Thule AB has supported a Ballistic Missile Early Warning System (BMEWS) radar 13 miles northeast of the airport. Early in its Cold War history, the runway supported frequent resupply flights, as well as SAC "Chrome Dome" missions, with B-52s laden with nuclear weapons on continuous airborne alert around the Northernmost perimeter of North America. On January 21, 1968, a B-52G (s/n 58-0188) on a "Chrome Dome" alert mission crashed into the sea ice roughly 7.5 miles west of the runway after attempting an emergency landing at Thule. The conventional explosives from the megaton-range thermonuclear warheads spread radioactive material over a large area. An early 1980s photograph of the base operations building at Sondrestrom AB, Greenland, displays the 1st Space Wing emblem, "the" Space Command logo, and the host unit 1015th Air Base Group. Sondrestrom supported transatlantic ferry flights and aerial refueling tankers in the early Cold War years, expanding support for the Distant Early Warning (DEW) Line of air defense radars and the building of the BMEWS radar at Thule AB. The last USAF personnel left the station in 1992, when the airport facilities were transferred to the local Danish government.

CHANGES THROUGHOUT THE EIGHTIES: The Passenger Terminal on Peterson AFB shows a good amount of snow cover on a typical Colorado winter day. In an early 1980s aerial view facing west, the expansion of Colorado Springs eastward shows the encroachment near Peterson AFB's perimeter. The Ent Building (1470) can be seen near the lower center right of the photograph. The area later containing building 1 (Hartinger Building), and later buildings 2 (Eberhard-Findley Building) and 3 (SMDC)—and the ample parking lot—is out of frame to the right.

PETERSON'S AIR FORCE RESERVE FLYING MISSION: A staple of nearly every military base in the 1980s was McDonald's, seen here at the intersection of Paine and Thule streets. Changing appetites of American consumers—and Peterson AFB members by extension—saw the McDonald's go out of business in the 2010s. As of 2023, the building holds Ghost Kitchens, supporting a number of small food establishments providing a variety of culinary choices. A 302nd Tactical Airlift Wing (TAW) C-130 comes in for a landing at Peterson AFB. The 731st Tactical Airlift Squadron (later, 731st Airlift Squadron) is the Air Force Reserve's only unit assigned the aerial firefighting mission using the U.S. Forest Service modular airborne firefighting system (MAFFS) equipment. The base has supported C-130 Hercules aircraft flown by 731st aircrews since 1982.

JOIN AIR FORCE SPACE COMMAND, AND COME SEE NEW YORK?: An aerial view of Verona Test Annex (NY), near Griffiss AFB shows the tell-tale clues of a space-related mission under the white geodesic domes. From 1989 to 1995, Verona was home to the 1st Space Surveillance Squadron, a 21 SW unit operating the low-altitude space surveillance (LASS) system gathering intelligence from space systems in near-Earth orbits. The test annex belonged to the Rome Air Development Center and supported engineering evaluation and operational testing of electromagnetic systems for the USAF. The lush green forests of southwest Germany backdrop the AN/GSC-52 high-capacity super high frequency (SHF) satellite communications terminal operated by the 3rd Space Communications Squadron (3 SCS) at Kapaun Air Station (DEU). The 3 SCS moniker was revived in 2022 as a subordinate unit to Space Delta 4 at Buckley SFB (CO), providing strategic and theater missile warning to the U.S. and international partners.

ETERNAL VIGILANCE FROM HOT, SANDY PLACES AROUND THE WORLD: The trucks of the 4th Space Warning Squadron (4 SWS) AN/MSQ-118 Mobile Ground Terminals (MGTs, colloquially known as "Midgets") sit at Holloman AFB (NM) within white gypsum sand dunes. During the 1970s, increasing accuracy of Soviet missiles placed several critical U.S. warfighting capabilities at risk. Planners at AFSPC designed mobile assets to increase the survivability of the Defense Support Program (DSP) missile warning system. The 1025th Satellite Communications Squadron (Mobile) activated in October 1983 at Holloman, reaching MGT initial operating capability in 1986. AFSPC transferred the MGTs to Greeley Air National Guard (ANG) Station (CO) in 1996, inactivating the renamed 4 SWS and reassigning the mission to the Colorado ANG's 137th Space Warning Squadron (137 SWS). The white geodesic domes at Joint Defence Facility Nurrungar, near Woomera (AUS), stand out from the red and brown sandy hills of South Australia. The facility was known as the DSP Overseas Ground Station (OGS) and became operational in 1971 with the 5th Joint Defense Space Communications Squadron (later renamed 5th Space Warning Squadron), until its closure in 1999. Today the site is abandoned, with two buildings and one geodesic dome remaining.

PAVE PAWS AND NUCLEAR-TIPPED CLAWS: An aerial shot of Cape Cod AFS (MA) shows the dual-face AN/FPS-115 PAVE PAWS (Phased Array Warning System) radar in 1986. The PAVE PAWS network of early warning radars was developed in the 1980s to detect and characterize submarine-launched ballistic missiles (SLBMs) on the continental U.S. Two sites were installed on the coasts—Beale AFB (west) and Cape Cod (east)—with two additional sites facing south (Eldorado AFS, TX) and southeast (Robins AFB, GA). The lessening probability of attack from the Gulf of Mexico or Southern azimuths saw the Texas and Georgia sites shut down in 1995. The Beale and Cape Cod sites were upgraded to the AN/FPS-132 Upgraded Early Warning Radar (UEWR) configuration in the 2000s and 2010s, respectively. The singular phased array face of the AN/FPQ-16 PARCS (Perimeter Acquisition Radar Attach Characterization System) at Cavalier Air Force Station (ND) vigilantly monitors the northern skies. The PARCS radar was originally the Perimeter Acquisition Radar (PAR) for the Safeguard Anti-Ballistic Missile System in the early 1970s. While the PAR would detect Soviet missiles, short-range Sprint and long-range LIM-49 Spartan nuclear-tipped interceptors would stop the incoming warheads. When the Anti-Ballistic Missile Treaty was signed in 1972, and Congress voted to shut down Safeguard in 1975, the PAR site was reactivated in 1977 for the early warning and space surveillance missions.

Remote Locations of Air Force Space Command: The Oscura Mountains on White Sands Missile Range (NM) backdrop the Ground-Based Electro-Optical Deep Space Surveillance (GEODSS) Experimental Test Site (ETS) on September 27, 1978. Operated by the Massachusetts Institute of Technology (MIT) Lincoln Laboratories, concepts developed at ETS helped evolve research & development projects into mature electro-optical technologies for space surveillance. ETS remained a testbed for electro-optical development as the GEODSS telescope network came online around the world, with the co-located Detachment 1 at WSMR achieving "first light" in 1982. Two USAF security policemen patrol the perimeter of the AN/FPS-108 COBRA DANE radar on Shemya AFS (AK) on October 23, 1984. The COBRA DANE radar replaced mechanical tracking radars in the late 1970s, monitoring Soviet missile tests on the Kamchatka Pennisula. Shemya's facilities were part of the transfer of assets from SAC to AFSPC in 1983. The base also serves as a diversion airport for civilian aircraft transiting the Pacific Ocean, fortuitously located at the tip of the Aleutian Islands.

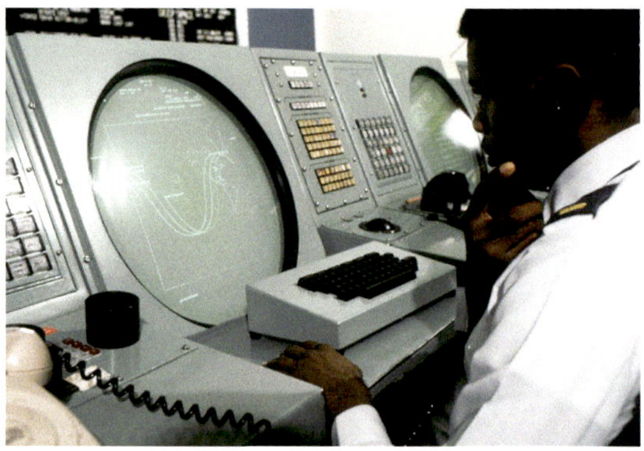

Eyes in the North Flows Data to the South: A view of three AN/FPS-50 early warning radar antennas and an antenna dome at the Ballistic Missile Early Warning System (BMEWS) Site 1 at Thule AB, Greenland, on October 24, 1984. The U.S. announced its decision to create BMEWS radars (Project 474L) at Thule and Clear AFS (Alaska) in January 1958, only months after the launch of Sputnik by the Soviet Union. The AN/FPS-50 system was deactivated in June 1987 and replaced by AN/FPS-120 Single-Sided Phased Array Radar Systems (SSPARS) to detect, track, and provides tactical warning and attack assessment of ballistic missiles launched against the U.S., Canada, and the United Kingdom. Second Lieutenant Freddie Stewart, orbital analyst in the Space Defense Operations Computation (SPADOC) Center inside Cheyenne Mountain, tracks the COSMOS 1402 breakup in February 1983. COSMOS 1402 was a Soviet radar ocean reconnaissance satellite with a nuclear reactor launched in August 1982, re-entering in January 1983 after the reactor was ejected. SPADOC personnel tracked friendly and adversary orbital objects with data provided by space surveillance and missile warning radars around the world.

5

Space Warriors at Peterson

After serving the USAAF as a storied World War II-era flying organization with bombers and fighters, the 21st Wing took to the Cold War skies with a cornucopia of jet fighters from the 1950s to the 1990s. After a brief inactivation period, the 21st activated again in Colorado Springs on May 15, 1992, absorbing the mission, personnel, and assets of recently inactivated 1st Space Wing and 3rd Space Support Wing. The newly designated 21st Space Wing (21 SW) assumed the missions of missile warning and space surveillance with a network of high-tech sensors built under the direction of Air Defense Command, Aerospace Defense Command, and Strategic Air Command since the early 1960s becoming the air force's premier operational organization in the space domain. The 21 SW became the USAF's most widespread and diverse wing, with fifteen weapon systems operated by forty-three diverse units, in twenty locations across five countries.

With the standup of the nation's sixth military service—United States Space Force (USSF)—old military echelons made way for new ways of thinking and organizing. The 21 SW was inactivated on July 24, 2020 and replaced by the Peterson-Schriever Garrison (P-S-GAR), along with the inactivation of the 21st Operations Group and 73rd Space Group, and being replaced by Space Delta 2 (Space Domain Awareness & Space Battle Management) and Space Delta 3 (Space Electromagnetic Warfare) respectively.

Responsibility for space-based missile warning units had previously transferred to the 460th Space Wing (460 SW) at Buckley AFB (CO) in 2004. The remaining 21 SW ground-based missile warning systems (PAVE PAWS, PARCS, UEWR) and 460 SW units were transferred to Space Delta 4 (Missile Warning), headquartered at the redesignated Buckley Space Force Base outside of Aurora, Colorado.

THE SPACE DEFENSE MISSION BECOMES MORE COMPLEX: The Peterson AFB entry sign on March 6, 1995 shows the commands and organizations resident on Peterson AFB: NORAD, USSPACECOM (1985), Air Force Space Command, and the 21 SW. The Space and Warning Systems Center (SWSC) managed the upkeep and development of mission-critical software—consisting of more than 12 million lines of code for thirty-four distinct operational systems written in twenty-seven different computer programming languages—that fulfilled operational requirements for NORAD and USSPACECOM.

SCUDs from the Skies: The Soviet Union developed the SS-1 "SCUD" battlefield missile during the 1950s, first seen during the 1957 May Day parade in Moscow. The weapon was a single-stage missile with a non-separating payload, an evolutionary upgrade from the German V-2 surface-to-surface missile. The MAZ-543 Transporter Erector Launcher (TEL) vehicle provided mobility for "shoot-and-scoot" tactics during Desert Storm, confounding Allied planners. The SS-1B SCUD could carry three types of warheads (chemical, nuclear, high explosive), causing concern with coalition planners based on Iraq's use of chemical weapons during the Iran-Iraq War (1980–1988). A total of eighty-eight SCUDs were launched into Saudi Arabia (forty-six) and Israel (forty-two) during Operations Desert Shield/Desert Storm. Use of DSP satellites to detect SCUD launches, led to the development of the Attack and Launch Early Reporting to Theater (ALERT) system by the 11th Space Warning Squadron (11 SWS).

AIR FORCE SPACE COMMAND'S "OLD MEN" GATHER, PART 1: Lt. Gen. Thomas S. Moorman, Jr., AFSPC commander, and his wife greet President George H. W. Bush upon his arrival at Peterson AFB on May 19, 1991, *en route* to the Air Force Academy graduation. In the background, Gen. Donald J. Kutyna, NORAD/USSPACECOM commander, greets First Lady Barbara Bush in the background. Below, former AFSPC commanders pose for a group photograph with the then-current commander, Lt. Gen. Thomas S. Moorman, Jr., (far right). From the left, the dignitaries included Gen. Donald J. Kutyna, Gen. Robert T. Herres, Gen. James V. Hartinger, and Maj. Gen. Maurice Padden. As a sidenote, Gen. Herres was selected in 1967 as a member of the Manned Orbiting Laboratory (MOL) Group 3, the air force's attempt at establishing a military astronaut cadre.

Emergency Responders are on the Way: A UH-60 Medivac helicopter from Fort Carson (CO) comes in for a landing at the site of a simulated aircraft crash, while a simulated casualty is loaded into an ambulance for transporting to a local hospital by Medical Group personnel and firemen. From February 13–17, 1996, emergency personnel from the Peterson Fire Department, Search & Recovery, Bioenvironmental, Mobile Command and Control Squadron and the 21st Medical Group all responded as part of the 21 SW Operational Readiness Inspection (ORI). The combined inspection tested Team Pete's ability to respond to battle conditions, power outages, mobility deployments, aircraft and automobile accidents, hostage situations, bomb threats, armed robbery, terrorism, and communication disruptions.

AERIAL DISPLAYS OVER COLORADO SPRINGS: On August 14, 1998, attendees of the AFSPC change-of-command ceremony between Gen. Howell M. Estes III (outgoing commander) and Gen. Richard B. Myers (incoming commander) saw a fly-over by a U.S. Navy F-14 Tomcat, USAF F-15 Eagle, Canadian Air Force CF-18 Hornet and a USAF F-16 Fighting Falcon. Air Chief Marshal Sir John Allison, Air Officer Commanding RAF Strike Command, arrives at Peterson AFB in an F-16D Fighting Falcon aircraft from Luke AFB (AZ) on October 30, 1998. The appearance of distinguished visitors is a common occurrence due to base's function as a nexus for command organizations such as AFSPC, USSPACECOM, and NORAD.

BRINGING FREQUENT VISITORS TO THE SPRINGS: A C-37A transporting Secretary of the Air Force F. Whitten Peters sits on the Peterson AFB ramp outside the passenger terminal on December 10, 1998. The C-37A are twin-engined, turbofan-equipped aircraft used for special airlift missions for high-ranking government and Department of Defense officials and is based upon the Gulfstream V aircraft. With Pikes Peak taking prominence in the image, VC-25A tail number 28000—better known as Air Force One—arrives at Peterson AFB on May 29, 1991 with President George H. W. Bush and the First Lady Barbara Bush. The VC-25 fleet is a frequent visitor to Team Pete, with presidents often attending the annual graduation ceremonies at the United States Air Force Academy.

A DAY IN THE LIFE OF TEAM PETE: Lt. Col. Mike Selva (center, left), on-scene commander, briefs Brig. Gen. Donald A. Streater (foreground, right), commander of the A-10 recovery operation, on the pararescuemen's progress at the crash site near Gold Dust Peak (CO) on July 8, 1997. On April 2, 1997, Capt. Craig Button took off on a live-ordnance training mission from Davis-Monthan AFB (AZ) with an A-10 Thunderbolt II attack aircraft. Button deviated from his flight plan and flew into the Rocky Mountains near Vail, Colorado, in an apparent suicide attempt. Recovery operations found aircraft wreckage and human remains, but four 500-lb. Mark 82 bombs remained unaccounted for. Security Forces team members from the 21st Security Forces Squadron practice firing their electronic M16 rifles using a combat arms training simulator on May 4, 1999. The squadron was participating in Guardian Challenge 99, the air force's premier space and missile competition.

VIPs at Peterson AFB: President of the United States William Jefferson Clinton holds a mirrored gift presented to him by the 1999 USAF Thunderbirds Aerial Demonstration Team with the VC-25A Air Force One presidential aircraft in the background on June 2, 1999. Commander of 21st Space Wing Brig. Gen. Jerry M. Drennan (left) speaks with USAF Chief of Staff Gen. Michael Ryan prior to his departure from Peterson AFB, CO, on September 2, 1999.

WHEN THE WORLD SHIFTED: Soldiers from the 3rd Infantry render honors as fire fighters and rescue workers unfurl a huge (20-foot by 38-foot) American flag over the side of the Pentagon as recovery efforts continued following the September 11, 2001 terrorist attack. The September 11, 2001 terrorist attacks on the World Trade Center and the Pentagon forever altered America's perceptions of safety in the modern world. Four commercial airliners were hijacked in the early morning hours, and used as weapons against planned targets in New York and Washington, D.C. Three planes struck their intended targets, while the fourth aircraft crashed in Shanksville, Pennsylvania, after the passengers attempted to retake control from the hijackers. In response to the attacks, a new defense playbook was written for North America, named Operation Noble Eagle. The NORAD commander was delegated more authority to investigate civilian aircraft incidents in the U.S. and Canada, and in 2002, U.S. Northern Command (USNORTHCOM)) was created, tasked with deterring, detecting, and defeating threats to U.S. soil.

U.S. Northern Command Activates in the Shadows of September 11, 2001: On October 6, 2003, Secretary of Defense Donald H. Rumsfeld and USAF Gen. Ralph Eberhart, commander of USNORTHCOM, talk with the senior military leadership at NORAD/NORTHCOM headquarters inside building 2 on Peterson AFB. Performing the trifecta of leadership jobs at Peterson, General Eberhart was commander-in-chief of NORAD, USSPACECOM (first iteration) commander, and commander of AFSPC during September 11, 2001. After the standup of USNORTHCOM and disestablishment of USSPACECOM, Gen. Eberhart took the reins of leadership for the defense of North America. President George W. Bush waves to onlookers as he exits Air Force One at Peterson Air Force Base on May 27, 2008. The president came to Colorado Springs to speak at the 50th Air Force Academy Graduation the following day. Bush told graduates, "Each of you gathered here this morning has answered that same call. I want to thank you for stepping forward to serve. The security of our citizens and the peace of the world will soon be in your hands—the best of hands. Be officers of character and integrity. Keep your wings level and true. Never falter; do not fail. And always know that America stands behind you."

THE AIR FORCE'S PREMIER SPACE AND MISSILE COMPETITION: First Lieutenant Ryan Collins (left), as mascot "The General" for the 50th Space Wing (Schriever AFB) engages in a spot of friendly swordplay with 21 SW mascot "Iron Mike" (S/Sgt. Barton Bosarge) during a break in the chef safety competition during Guardian Challenge 2001, held at Vandenberg AFB (CA). Guardian Challenge is a four-day event hosted annually at Vandenberg to recognize the best and demonstrate AFSPC's warfighting skills across operations, maintenance, security, and support specialties. On May 5, 1999, four 21 SW security forces team members race for the finish line during Guardian Challenge 99.

PEERING THROUGH THE HEAVENS, OUT UNDER NEW MEXICO SKIES: The constellation Orion (center, three stars in a row) is nearly hidden in this view of the nighttime skies over Detachment 1, 21st Space Wing's GEODSS site at White Sands Missile Range (WSMR), New Mexico. In 1982, the New Mexico GEODSS site was the first to reach initial operating capability (IOC), with other GEODSS telescopes in Hawaii, Diego Garcia, and South Korea following suit. Being some of the most accurate and sensitive optical telescopes in the world, the GEODSS optical network can track objects as small as a basketball out to 20,000 miles. Maj. Erin Salinas inspects one of Det 1's telescopes before mission tasking begins. The WSMR site is unique as it is co-located with Lincoln Laboratory's Experimental Test Site (ETS), the testbed for GEODSS technologies.

Preparing for the Electromagnetic Battlefield: Members of the Peterson's space control units perform operations checks on satellite communications (SATCOM) equipment both in garrison and while deployed to Southwest Asia. These satellite antennae are first-line systems in an on-going conflict for control of the electromagnetic spectrum. With thousands of frequencies to monitor over a continuous spectrum in various communications bands, the U.S. Air Force, and now Space Force warriors have a challenging task of identifying, tracking, and defending this limited resource for U.S. and allied force operations.

ABANDON ALL HOPE: Members of the 1st Expeditionary Space Control Squadron (1 ESPCS) third rotation pose for a picture atop their control center in late 2010. Outside the 1ESPCS operations compound, a subtle warning to visitors comes from Dante's *Inferno*, one of the famous passages from medieval literature. As Dante passes through the gate of Hell, he sees an inscription with the phrase "*Lasciate ogne speranza, voi ch'intrate*," translated as "Abandon all hope, ye who enter here." The 1 ESPCS was made up of operators and maintenance members from the 4th and 76th Space Control Squadrons assigned to the 21 SW.

Defending the Spectrum while "Doin' the Deid": Squadron members of the 17th Expeditionary Space Control Squadron (17 ESPCS)—led by Lt. Col. Joel "Oz" Bieberle (center, smiling)—pose for a photo in front of their weapons system in 2015 at Al Udeid Air Base, Qatar. The 17 ESPCS morale patch shows an ever-vigilant wolf, ears perked up to monitor for threats, in desert camouflage colors with an unintelligible Arabic script at the bottom.

RETURNING HOME TO COLORADO SPRINGS: Members of Peterson's space control community disembark a C-5 Galaxy to greet their families at Peterson AFB on August 13, 2016. Col. John Shaw, 21 SW commander, welcomes Maj. Christian Pierce back to Colorado Springs. Maj. Pierce commanded an expeditionary space control unit for a ninety-day rotational assignment in Southwest Asia.

SHINING EXAMPLES OF 21ST SPACE WING LEADERSHIP: Following 21 SW commander Brig. Gen. John Shaw's promotion ceremony, retired Gen. Gene Renaurt (far left), Gen. John Hyten, AFSPC commander, Tonia Shaw (center), Brig. Gen. John Shaw, and Mr. Peter Teets (far right), former undersecretary of the air force, pose for a photo. Then-Col. Shaw commanded the 21 SW from 2013 2015 and transferred to Offutt AFB (NE) as deputy director for U.S. Strategic Command (USSTRATCOM). Shaw would later transfer to the United States Space Force in 2020. Members of the Peterson Community remember 21 SW commander Col. Thomas Falzarano, who died unexpectedly in his home in May 2020. Falzarano was known for his "TDY for a Day" entries on the base website, where he would engage with members under his command at various locations around Colorado Springs and at 21 SW geographically separated units.

AIRBORNE FIRE FIGHTERS: An Air Force Reserve 302nd Airlift Wing (302 AW) C-130 (s/n 94-7319) has Modular Aerial Firefighting Systems (MAFFS) equipment installed at Peterson AFB. During fire season, 302 AW aircraft marked with bright orange "2" and "5" numbers on their tails and fuselage stand twelve-hour shifts for seven to twelve days. The MAFFS mission requires aircraft to fly at low altitudes when targeting wildfires. The MAFFS-equipped C-130s can carry 3,000 gallons of fire retardant which can be completely discharged in under five seconds or it can be spread across multiple airdrops, covering an area one-quarter of a mile long and 100 feet wide. Airmen test the functionality of a 302 AW Modular Airborne Firefighting System unit loaded inside the cargo bay of a C-130H aircraft on August 2, 2023. The USAF maintains four MAFFS units nationwide, with three belonging to the Air National Guard—the 145 AW (North Carolina), 153 AW (Wyoming), and 146 AW (California)

NEW FORCE, NEW PARADIGMS, NEW SYMBOLS: The USSF heraldic emblems for Space Delta 3 and the 4th Electromagnetic Warfare Squadron (EWS). The stand-up of USSF shifted the paradigm of service echelons and unit organization. Gone were the terms "wing," "group," "numbered air force" from the aerial-focused service. The organization of USSF's echelons retained the use of "squadron," but shifted the next echelon up to a "delta," symbolizing change and innovation and evoking historic ties to the earliest days of the USAF space community. The 4 EWS—formerly the 4th Space Control Squadron (4 SPCS)—trains, equips, and mobilizes to employ space electromagnetic warfare capabilities for the commander USSPACECOM and other joint force commanders to support full spectrum national security objectives. The 4 EWS has a storied history starting with support to the Cold War-era Electronic Security Command (1986–1990) and Air Force Space Command (1990–2019), residing in austere locations ranging from Texas to New Mexico. On April 15, 2022, 4 SPCS was redesignated as the 4th Electromagnetic Warfare Squadron.

OPPOSITE PAGE
UPGRADED SYSTEMS AND NEW EDUCATIONAL OPPORTUNITIES: On March 12, 2020, USSF Guardians from the 4th Space Control Squadron (4 SPCS) accepted the handover of the first Block 10.2 configuration of the Counter Communications System (CCS) space electronic warfare (SEW) system on Peterson AFB (CO). First introduced in 2004, the Counter Communications System provides joint force commanders with the ability to reversibly deny adversary satellite communications across the full spectrum of conflict. Since its introduction, the transportable space electronic warfare system has undergone two major system upgrades (Block 10.1 and Block 10.2) and is currently operated by active-duty units, as well as Air National Guard units in California, Colorado, Florida, and Hawaii. The Moorman Space Education and Training Center houses the National Security Space Institute, charged with providing space professional military education to the military space professionals in the United States and its allies. The center is named after Gen. Thomas S. Moorman, Jr., commander of Air Force Space Command (1990–1992) and USAF vice chief of staff (1994–1997).

THE MOORMAN
SPACE EDUCATION
AND
TRAINING CENTER
1876

AIR FORCE SPACE COMMAND'S "OLD MEN" GATHER, PART 2: Gen. Kevin P. Chilton, commander of Air Force Space Command fires an M-4 rifle as a 21 SW security forces member looks on. Joining the USAF as a F-4 and F-15 fighter pilot, Chilton completed Test Pilot School in 1984, before being assigned to the National Aeronautics and Space Administration (NASA) as an astronaut. Chilton flew on STS-49 (1992), STS-59 (1994), and STS-76 (1996) before returning to the USAF in 1998. He served as AFSPC commander from 2006 to 2007, before being nominated as commander of United States Strategic Command (USSTRATCOM). Former AFSPC commanders gather inside Building 1. Front row (R to L): Generals Charles Horner (1992–1994); Howell M. Estes III (1996–1998); Donald J. Kutyna (1987–1990; 1992); C. Robert Kehler (2007–2011); Richard Myers (1998–2000); Thomas Moorman, Jr. (1990–1992); Ralph Eberhart (2000–2002). Back row (R to L): Chief Master Sergeant Richard T. Small; General Lance W. Lord; Major General Thomas Deppe

LEADERSHIP FOR THE NATION'S NEWEST SPACE ORGANIZATIONS: Gen. John "Jay" Raymond, last AFSPC commander, speaks during the 21 SW's twenty-fifth anniversary dinner at The Club, May 26, 2017. Raymond was the 21 SW commander from 2008–2009, with prior stints under the 21 SW as commander of the 5th Space Surveillance Squadron at RAF Feltwell (UK) in 2000. With the standup of the USSF on December 20, 2019, Raymond became the first chief of space operations (CSO), and the lead guardian for approximately 8600 service personnel. U.S. Army Gen. James H. Dickinson was the second commander (2020–2024) of the second iteration of USSPACECOM, the eleventh and newest unified combatant command. Dickinson assumed command on August 20, 2020, after serving as the first deputy commander of USSPACECOM, under Gen. Jay Raymond.

The Scars of September 11:

One of the recommendations from congressional investigations during the months after the September 11 terrorist attacks on the United States was the creation of a Combatant Command with the mission of providing command and control for Department of Defense (DOD) homeland defense efforts and to coordinate defense support of civil authorities. U.S. Northern Command (USNORTHCOM) was established October 1, 2002, with an area of responsibility including air, land, and sea approaches encompassing the continental United States, Canada, Mexico, and the surrounding water out to approximately 500 nautical miles. Peterson AFB's building 2 constructed in 2002—dedicated as the Eberhard-Findley Building—contains the headquarters to USSNORTHCOM and NORAD. The 9-11 Memorial outside of building 2 dedicated on May 18, 2010 is comprised of three parts—the recovered steel beam pays respect to the lives lost in New York and points in the city's direction; the five-sided planter honors those who died at the Pentagon; and the soil in the planter comes from Pennsylvania to pay respect to the people who died on Flight 93, which crashed in Shanksville (PA).

THE SUN NEVER SETS ON THE 21ST SPACE WING: This economic impact graphic shows the impact of operations coordinated and controlled from Peterson, exemplifying "The Sun never sets on the 21st Space Wing." On July 26, 2021, United States Space Force renamed Schriever AFB, Peterson AFB, and Cheyenne Mountain AFS to reflect their administration by USSF. The names changes were part of an overall initiative by the Department of the Air Force to establish a unique identity and culture within the USSF, and accurately reflecting the important space missions performed by airmen and guardians stationed at the newly renamed Schriever Space Force Base, Peterson Space Force Base, and Cheyenne Mountain Space Force Station.

DELTAS AND HYDRAS: The logo of Space Base Delta 1 (SBD 1), headquartered at Peterson SFB, shows a six-headed hydra representing the six worldwide locations supported by the organization's administration. SBD 1 is responsible for Peterson SFB, Schriever SFB, and Cheyenne Mountain SFS in Colorado, Pituffik Space Base (formerly Thule Air Base) in Greenland, New Boston SFS in New Hampshire, and Kaena Point SFS in Hawaii. SBD 1 was formerly known as the Peterson-Schriever Garrison (P-S-GAR) until its redesignation to Space Base Delta 1 on May 23, 2022. P-S GAR was activated on July 24, 2020, replacing the 21st Space Wing and the 50th Space Wing. Appropriately, the red carpet leading to the Peterson passenger terminal now represents the base's current designation as a Space Force Base.

6

Peterson Air and Space Museum

Currently one of only twelve field museums in the United States Air Force Heritage Program, the Edward J. Peterson Air and Space Museum did not always exist in its current form. In 1975, Col. Donald Parson, 46th Aerospace Defense Wing commander, established the NORAD Visitor Center in the present-day museum buildings, becoming the start and end location to all public tours to the Cheyenne Mountain Complex. The center also obtained static displays and exhibits on NORAD's mission. On April 28, 1981, Col. Glen Griffith, 46th Aerospace Defense Wing commander, officially established the Edward J. Peterson Air and Space Museum after receiving Air Staff approval to include it within the Air Force Heritage Program. When the 21st Space Wing was activated in 1992, the museum was aligned as a wing staff agency, receiving appropriate host unit support. (*Author's collection*)

Lieutenant Peterson's Life in Pieces: A museum mannequin of Lt. Edward J. Peterson, Jr. welcomes visitors to "his" museum. Inside the main museum buildings, artifacts and photographs of Peterson's short life sit within glass display cases. Other exhibits within the main museum building include artifacts from Colorado Springs Army Air Base's earliest assigned units, such as PROTU and the 6th Photographic Squadron. Bits of ephemera, such as PROTU staff car license plate and an early 1940s Christmas card from the base, inform museum visitors of the important work done at the base during World War II. The 6 PS mascot "Nicky the Owl" also informs visitors of the critical photoreconnaissance and mapping work performed there. (*Author's collection*)

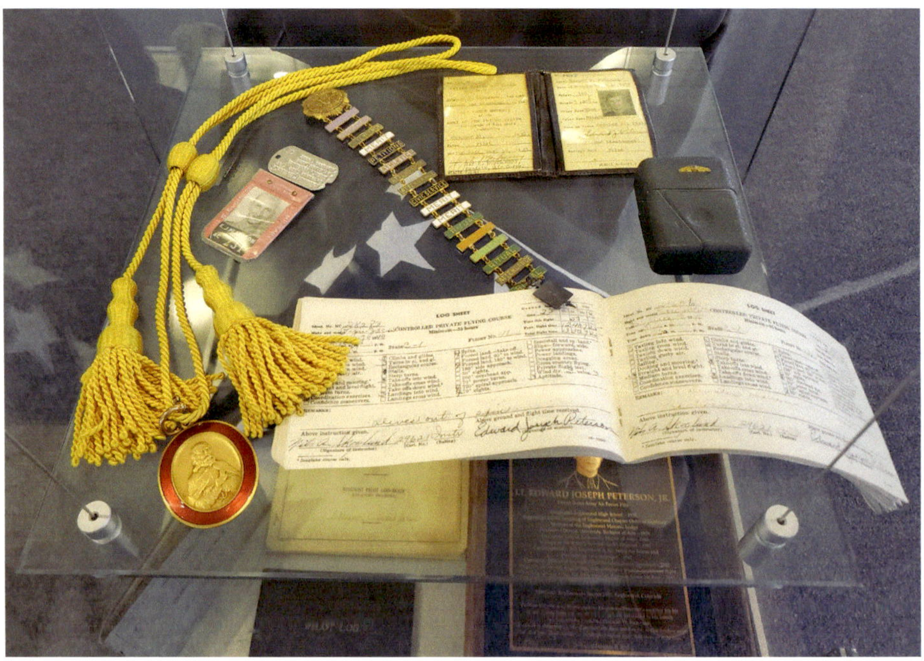

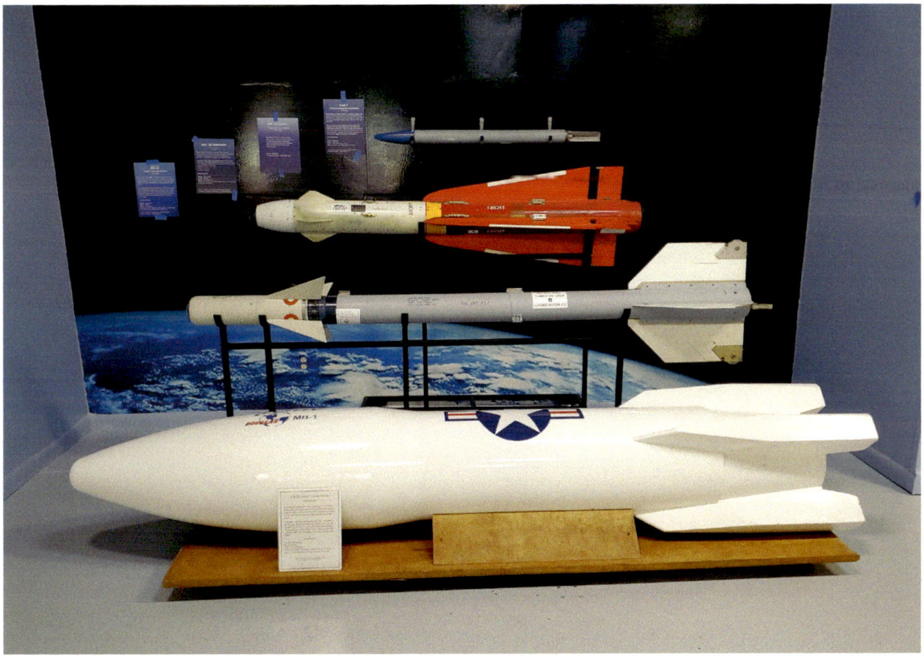

Air Defense Aerial Artifacts: As the former headquarters of Air (and later, Aerospace) Defense Command, the museum showcases air-to-air weapons used by fighter-interceptor aircraft during the Cold War, such as these examples. From bottom to top: AIR-2A Genie nuclear-tipped rocket; AIM-9B Sidewinder missile; AIM-4D Falcon missile; Mark 4 "Mighty Mouse" 2.75-inch folding-fin aerial rocket. A Republic P-47N Thunderbolt (s/n 44-89425) nicknamed "Wild Hair," is moved into position by volunteers inside the Old City Hangar, the oldest structure in the museum complex. (*Author's collection/USAF*)

Cacophony of Colors: Uniforms worn by generations of missile combat crew members are on display inside the Old City Hangar near the intercontinental ballistic missile (ICBM) exhibits. While the mannequins' faces look like Uncle Fester, an emo teenager, and a shopping mall model the uniforms are wholly representative of the 448th Strategic Missile Squadron (left), 400th Strategic Missile Squadron (center), and 392nd Training Squadron (right) uniforms. A headless museum mannequin wears a blue ascot bearing the emblem of the 1st Space Wing, headquartered at Peterson from 1983 to 1992. This ascot was worn by all service members assigned to the unit during the early '80s. (*Author's collection*)

NORAD UNIFORMS: Representative of their unique mission of defending North American airspace, crews working within the Cheyenne Mountain Complex wore grey flight suits, with rank affixed to epaulets on the shoulders. This uniform was worn by USAF S/Sgt. John W. Clark, who worked in the Battle Staff from 1990 to 1993. The shoulder patch represents the Cheyenne Mountain Operations Center, while the chest patches represent NORAD and USSPACECOM (first iteration, 1985–2002). Next to the CMAFS flight suit is a Canadian Armed Forces "CF Greens." When the armed services of Canada were unified into the Canadian Armed Forces in 1968, the adopted uniform consisted of a set of rifle green colored pants and a single-breasted four-button tunic in this equivalent of a business suit meant for ordinary duty.

INSIDE THE GRANITE STRONGHOLD, PART 1: Stemming from the Peterson Museum's lineage as the NORAD visitors center, the present-day collection includes many artifacts from the Cheyenne Mountain Complex. The Cheyenne Mountain Upgrade model from 1989 shows the changes made to the operations buildings during the upgrade program dubbed Granite Sentry.

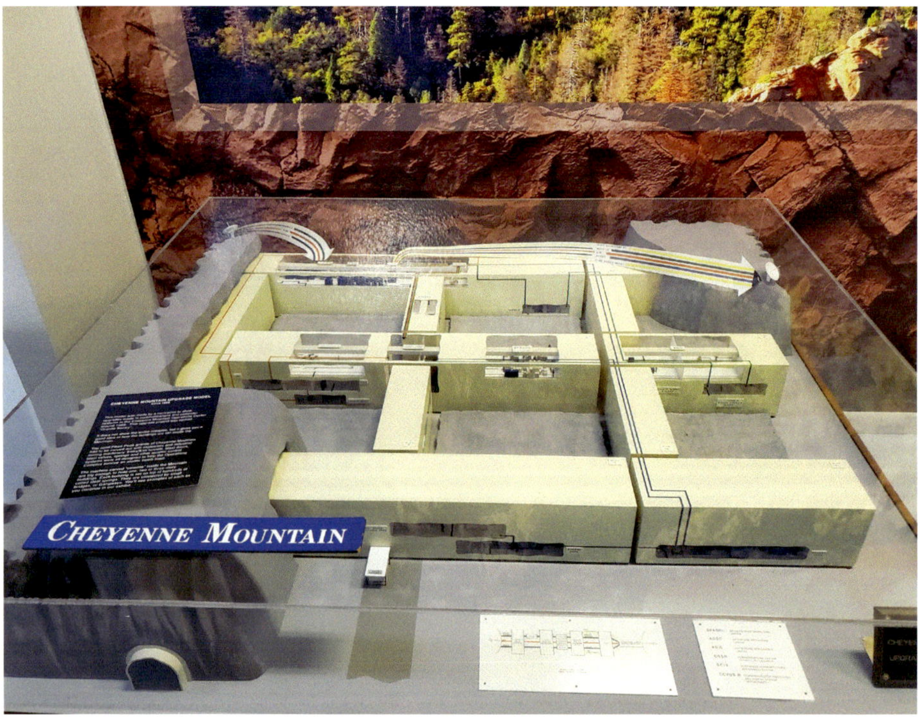

Inside the Granite Stronghold, Part 2:

The Red Phone on display had a direct connection to the White House to inform the president's staff of any attacks on the United States. No dialing was required—just lift the receiver and the phone on the other end would ring. The steel spring assembly on display is just one of over 1,300 used to support the buildings inside Cheyenne Mountain. Each spring can support more than 1,000 pounds and provides the ability for the buildings inside the mountain to flex 12 inches in any direction.

Reach out and Nuke Someone:

The Peterson Museum provides a rare comparative look at two sides of the ICBM mission: munitions maintenance and operations. The museum has a titanium shroud from the LGM-118A Peacekeeper (PK) ICBM alongside a Single Re-entry Vehicle (SRV) deployment module from the LGM-30G Minuteman III (MM3) variant. Nominally PK could carry either six or ten Mark (Mk) 21 warheads, while MM3 had a maximum of three Mk 12/12A warheads. Modernization requirements as well as strategic arms control treaties saw the MM3 force drop from three down to one warhead per missile, replacing Mk 12/12A RVs with the Mk 21 RV. The Missile Procedure Trainer instructed PK missileers (stationed only at F.E. Warren AFB) on their weapon system from 1986 to 2005.

TOOLS OF THE MISSILEER TRADE: The Strategic Automated Command and Control System (SACCS) required two 8-inch floppy disks to load a minimal operating system prior to message receipt or transmission. While top-of-the-line when introduced in the 1970s, the floppy disk supply chain was extinct by the twenty-first century with remaining examples only found in museums. In 2019, this outdated method of magnetic storage was supplanted by modern (*circa* 2010s) digital storage technology. The red metal box above the console, complete with two combination locks, held the authentication cards for nuclear weapon employment. Called the SAS (Sealed Authenticator System) container, this box held the means to authenticate a nuclear launch order originating from the National Command Authority. Each crewmember had to independently verify the orders, then take their lock off the SAS container, obtaining the materials within.

AIR DEFENSE FIGHTERS THROUGH THE DECADES: The introduction of the F-15 Eagle into the U.S. inventory in 1974 was a watershed moment for aerial combat. The all-weather, extremely maneuverable air superiority fighter brought its sizeable weapons load and advanced avionics to the North American air defense mission in the 1980s. Air Defense Command (later Air Defense–Tactical Air Command), operated four F-15 squadrons at Minot AFB (ND), Langley AFB (VA), NAS Keflavik (Iceland), and McChord AFB (WA), until the end of the Cold War. The air defense mission was transferred to the Air National Guard and First Air Force on October 1, 1995, with a sizable fleet of Eagles to defend the nation. The Avro CF-100 Canuck (right foreground), sitting in front of an EC-121 Warning Star (left, rear), was the only Canadian-designed and built fighter aircraft to go into large-scale production, entering service in 1953. Nine Royal Canadian Air Force CF-100 squadrons—armed with eight 0.50-caliber machine guns and fifty-eight 2.75-inch rockets—defended North America's northern approach until 1962, when Canucks were converted into electronic warfare assets until their phaseout in the 1970s.

CARING FOR HISTORIC AIRCRAFT: Maintenance workers repainted the CF-188 (also known as the CF-18) Hornet at the Peterson Air and Space Museum on October 13, 2022. In 1977, the Canadian government identified a requirement to replace the CF-101 Voodoo, CF-104 Starfighter, and CF-116 Freedom Fighter (Northrop F-5) for various air defense missions. The Grumman F-14 and McDonnell Douglas F-15 were considered contenders but rejected due to their high purchase costs. The Hornet provided two engines for reliability, excellent airborne radar, and a more affordable price tag. One hundred and thirty-eight CF-18s were procured from 1982 to 1988, at a total capital cost of $4 billion in 1982 dollars ($12.6 billion in 2023). The EC-121 Warning Star sits as the centrepiece at the Peterson Museum's air and space park.

AERIAL MENAGERIE IN COLORADO SPRINGS: Vestiges of North American air defense sit within the grounds of the Peterson Air and Space Museum awaiting visitors to hear their stories. Two stalwart air defenders—a CIM-10A BOMARC missile and F-94C Starfire—are a small sample of the weapon systems available to visitors. Nuclear-tipped BOMARC missiles operated from 1959 to 1972 at nine sites in the CONUS and two in Canada. After decommissioning as air defense weapons, BOMARCs became high-speed targets for live-fire weapon testing. The F-94C Starfire had a short operational life as an air defender (1949 to 1959) and limited usefulness with its lack of an aircraft gun (C-model), relying on short-range unguided rockets. Both systems, however, filled a critical gap during the early days of the Cold War.

Bibliography

Boyne, W. J., "Carbon Copy Bomber," *Air Force* magazine. Washington, D.C.: Air Force Association, 2009, www.airandspaceforces.com/article/0609bomber/

Dudney, R. S., "Namesakes: Edward J. Peterson," *Air Force* magazine. Washington, D.C.: Air Force Association, 2020, www.airandspaceforces.com/article/namesakes-edward-peterson-jr/

Hoffecker, J. F., Whorton, M., and Buechler, C. R., "Cold War Historic Properties of the 21st Space Wing." Peterson AFB, CO: Air Force Space Command History Office, 1996

Maurer, Maurer, (ed.) "Combat Squadrons of the Air Force, World War II." Washington, D.C.: Office of Air Force History, 1982, media.defense.gov/2010/Dec/02/2001329899/-1/-1/0/AFD-101202-002.pdf.

Shaw, F. J., (ed.) "Locating Air Force Base Sites: History's Legacy." Washington, D.C.: Air Force History and Museums Program, 2004, www.amc.af.mil/Portals/12/documents/AFD-131018-055.pdf.

About the Peterson Air and Space Museum

The Edward J. Peterson, Jr., Air and Space Museum is one of only twelve USAF field museums, proudly preserving and displaying historic items about its namesake and the various organizations and military units on Peterson SFB. The museum is located right in the center of an 8.3-acre historic district which includes the original Colorado Springs Municipal Airport passenger terminal, City Hangar, Broadmoor Hangar, and an award-winning airpark. All of Colorado Springs' original Municipal Airport buildings are listed on the National Register of Historic Places and as part of a Colorado-designated state historic district.

Exterior displays include:
- F-15 Eagle
- F-106 Delta Dart
- CF-188
- EC-121 Warning Star
- MIM-14 Nike-Hercules Missile
- CIM-10 BOMARC

Interior displays include:
- The life and death of Lieutenant Edward J. Peterson, Jr.
- Early Colorado Springs aviation history
- Air defense of North America
- Cheyenne Mountain Complex
- Staff Sergeant Jose R. "Mark" Aragon and Vietnam warriors

The museum is free and open to the public, however, visitors without base access must request access at the Visitor Control Center at least three business days prior to the intended visit date. Details on obtaining base access and scheduling can be found on the museum website (petemuseum.org).

Contacting the Museum:

Mailing Address: 150 E. Ent Avenue Peterson SFB, CO 80914-1303
Phone: 719-556-5543
Email: staff@petemuseum.org
Hours: Tuesday–Friday, 10 a.m. to 3 p.m.
Closed Saturday–Monday and U.S. Federal Holidays

Decimal:	38.82275739883	-104.70260085934
DMS:	38°49'21.9"N	104°42'09.4"W

Index

About the Author

Joseph T. Page II ("Joe") is a military historian and former air force officer. The military history "bug" bit him early in life while growing up at White Sands Missile Range, New Mexico, the "Birthplace of America's Missile and Space Activity." After spending a decade in uniform, Joe and his family finally settled in Albuquerque, New Mexico. He holds degrees in English and history from the University of New Mexico.